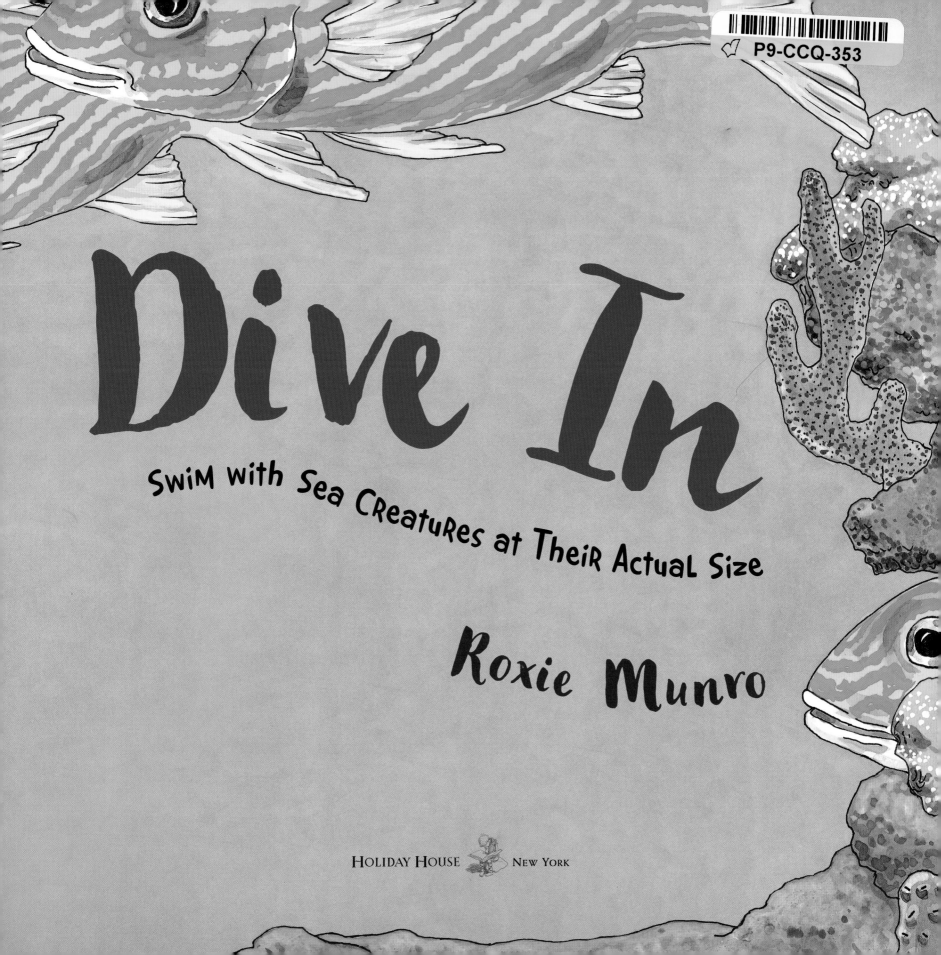

Dive In

Swim with Sea Creatures at Their Actual Size

Roxie Munro

HOLIDAY HOUSE · NEW YORK

INTRODUCTION

Coral reefs are magical—full of life and color and motion, and even sound. Although they cover less than 1% of the earth's surface, they are home to more than a quarter of all marine fish species, as well as sea stars, octopi, tube worms, sea urchins, sponges, and other fascinating creatures. There may be more than one million different species of plants and animals living in coral reefs. Because coral reefs have such a rich diversity of life, they are sometimes called the rainforests of the ocean.

A coral reef is formed very slowly by the limestone skeletons of thousands and thousands of polyps, tiny simple creatures related to anemones and jellyfish. Each new generation builds on top of the skeletons of the older ones. Colonies of coral make all sorts of elaborate, brightly colored structures, with fun names like brain coral, yellow sea whip, lettuce coral, orange pipe, and elephant ear.

Created in shallow warm water in tropical oceans around the equator, coral reefs are found along coastlines and near volcanic islands. They rise to or near the ocean's surface in the form of fringing reefs, which grow close to the shore; barrier reefs, which grow farther from the shore and are separated by a channel; or atolls, which are islands made of coral that are sometimes formed on the rim of extinct volcanos. I've visited coral reefs in Hawaii, French Polynesia in the South Pacific, and the Caribbean, where the creatures shown in this book live.

SPOTTED CLEANER SHRIMP are *crustaceans*, animals with a hard outer shell. These tiny, patterned shrimp live safely among stinging sea anemones. The shrimp swishes its antennae to attract fish, and then dines on the *parasites* and flakes of loose skin it removes from the fish. It even enters the mouth of some fish and doesn't get eaten!

Except for the dwarf angelfish, the **ROCK BEAUTY** is the smallest marine angelfish in the Atlantic. It is thin bodied with a roundish profile and is distinguished from butterflyfish, which is a similar fish family, by a sharp spine sticking out of its cheek. It goes by the names corn sugar, rock beasty, and yellow nanny as well. Rock beauties form longtime *monogamous* relationships and are *territorial*—they like to stay in one neighborhood.

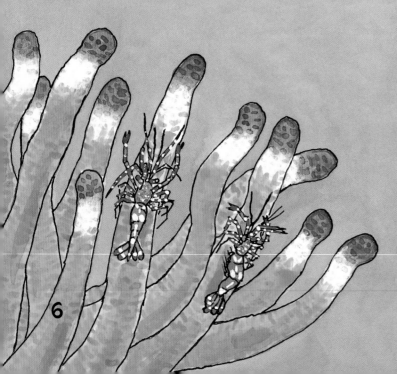

The SPOTTED TRUNKFISH is a boxfish. It has a bony outer surface like body armor and, because of its rigid bulky shape, is a slow swimmer. Trunkfish exude a colorless slime-like toxin from their skin when touched. The poison is dangerous only when swallowed. But even large *predators*, like sharks, can die from eating a trunkfish.

The beautiful BATWING CORAL CRAB is the largest marine crab in the Caribbean Sea. Like shrimp and lobsters, these crabs are crustaceans. They get their name from their wide arms, which look like bat wings. With four pairs of legs, they can move rapidly sideways.

The elongated TRUMPETFISH can swiftly change color to *camouflage* itself and blend into the background. It often hides among sea fan coral, pipe sponges, and sea whips, floating snout down. A trumpetfish can open its mouth as wide as its body and suck down prey quickly, like a vacuum cleaner.

Instead of holding hands, male and female LONGSNOUT SEAHORSES hold tails. The male then shows off by changing colors and gracefully swimming around the female. Together they dance and "kiss," swimming snout to snout. They remain partners for life. There are at least forty-seven different seahorse species. They range in size from a half inch to a foot long.

This TWO-SPINED SEA STAR isn't a fish because it doesn't have a backbone. It's an *echinoderm*, which has a hard internal skeleton and spiny skin. Most sea stars, which are also called starfish, have five arms, but some have up to fifty. The arms are amazing: If one gets chopped off, another one grows; and there is an eye at the end of each. Sea stars crawl slowly, using hundreds of tiny tube feet on the underside of each arm.

SPOTTED MORAY EELS can grow up to four feet long. They like to hide in dark recesses. Moray eels constantly open and close their mouths. This is not to look fierce, but to breathe by moving water through their gills for respiration. At least thirteen other species of moray eels live in the Caribbean, including green, purple mouth, viper, goldentail, stout, and honeycomb morays.

RAINBOW PARROTFISH have a tough parrot-like beak with fused teeth that they use to scrape algae from coral. They use a second set of teeth in their throat to grind up the coral they eat. They expel coral they can't digest as sand. A single parrotfish can turn a ton of coral into sand every year! Another unique thing about these fish is that some can change their sex. Extra-brightly colored parrotfish, like this one, are males that used to be females.

FRENCH GRUNTS often swim in large schools, numbering in the thousands. Their name comes from the sound they make to chase away predators. They use their teeth to make a grinding noise that is magnified by a special air bladder. Their nicknames include banana grunt and redmouth grunt.

The small **FOUR-EYED BUTTERFLYFISH** has a big black spot near its tail to fool attackers into thinking that the front of its body is the back end. They flit around coral like a butterfly, often in pairs, looking for tiny shellfish for dinner.

QUEEN ANGELFISH get their name from the "crowns" on their foreheads. They are also known for the unusual cleaning stations set up by the young fish along the reef. At these stations there is a truce between predators and prey, and small fish trust larger fish not to eat them. Predator fish remain motionless as small queen angelfish remove parasites from their bodies.

The **SERGEANT MAJOR'S** name comes from its vertical stripes, or bars, which resemble the traditional insignia of the military rank of sergeant major. During the day these fish stay together and swim and feed in schools of hundreds. But at night they scatter into caves and holes in the reef. Sergeant majors are bossy and aggressive when guarding their nests.

The **QUEEN TRIGGERFISH** got the name "trigger" because of the clever way it protects itself. At night it can raise and lock spines on its fins to wedge itself into a crevice so predators can't pull it out. It can unlock the spines when it wants to leave. Its small mouth has strong jaws with powerful incisor-like teeth that can chisel holes in hard-shelled prey, such as crabs.

The **REEF SHARK'S** ancestors have been around for more than 400 million years—before dinosaurs roamed the earth. Sharks don't have any bones. Their skeletons are made of *cartilage*, like your ears and nose. Cartilage is not as hard as bone, but it is stiffer than muscles. Reef sharks have lots of sharp teeth lined up in rows; when one breaks off, a new one takes its place. Reef sharks are the most common sharks on coral reefs, but nurse sharks, whale sharks, sand tigers, and the great hammerheads sometimes visit.

SLENDER FILEFISH are shy.
They often float head down and use camouflage
to hide among soft corals. In seconds, they can
change color to match the coral. Other types of
Caribbean filefish include unicorn, scrawled,
orange-spotted, fringed, and pygmy.

As you can see, **LONGSPINE SQUIRRELFISH** have large squirrel-like eyes. They make two kinds of sounds: a single grunt to defend territory and a short staccato burst to show alarm. Like birds, squirrelfish have a behavior called mobbing. When they hear the staccato sound, they first dash into crevices and then come out in big groups making more staccato sounds to scare away predators such as moray eels.

The **STRIATED FROGFISH** has a thin elongated fin above its snout that tips forward and acts as a fishing rod with a lure on the end to attract prey. Usually the frogfish quietly waits until a fish or a crab ventures near and then gobbles it up in an amazing feat. It moves quickly and can open its jaws incredibly wide—up to twelve times the mouth's original size. Frogfish can swallow a fish almost twice their size. They can also change color to camouflage themselves against the ocean floor.

The **SPOTTED SCORPIONFISH'S** wild textures, large head, and colorful markings make it a master of camouflage. A sit-and-wait ambush predator like the frogfish, it lies motionless on the coral reef, waiting to swallow small fish and crustaceans whole in one big gulp.

The little **LONGSNOUT BUTTERFLYFISH** picks small *invertebrates* out of tiny holes and from between sea urchins' spines. It's so fast, it can grab a tube worm before the worm can pull back into its tube. The fins on its sides work like oars to brake, sprint, turn, and even go backward.

REEF SQUIDS communicate
by changing colors to signal messages
such as alarm or an interest in mating
to other nearby squids. They can even show
two patterns at once. They might show camouflage
on their right side while sending a message
on their left side. Like their octopus cousins,
squids have eight arms. But they also have two long tentacles,
with suckers at the end to grab prey and pull it in toward their beak.

The **SOUTHERN STINGRAY** has a *venomous* jagged barb at the base of its tail that it uses to stab predators. Rays gracefully glide across the bottom of the sea floor, flapping their wide wing-like fins. They often lie partially hidden in the sand, with just their big eyes showing. They are in the same family as sharks and have skeletons made of cartilage instead of bones. Like sharks, their strong teeth can crush *mollusks* like clams, mussels, and oysters.

ATLANTIC BLUE TANGS have a unique defense system. At the base of their tail is a yellow fin that it can move, called the caudal spine. This sharp knife-like fin pops out when the fish is excited or threatened. Tangs can attack predators with the caudal spine by whipping their tails or thrashing sideways.

FAIRY BASSLETS hang out, often upside down or on their sides, under ledges or in crevices. Although these brightly colored creatures are among the smallest fish around the reef, their size matters. The largest male rules the group.

The **SPINY LOBSTER** is a crustacean. Its shell is a skeleton on the outside of its body. Lobsters shed their shells as their bodies grow. Their old shells split open to reveal soft new skeletons that harden in a day or two.

NASSAU GROUPERS have large lips and mouths full of small, roughly textured teeth for holding onto prey. They're among the largest fish in the Caribbean, and some groupers, like the goliath, can grow up to eight feet long.

Little **YELLOW NOSE GOBIES** operate reef cleaning stations. Their clients are larger fish. Tiny gobies remove and then eat parasites, algae, and loose skin from the larger fish. This keeps the big fish healthy and gives the gobies their dinner.

The **COMMON OCTOPUS** is a mollusk, as are snails, clams, and squids. Like the squid, an octopus also changes colors and patterns to camouflage itself. An octopus has excellent vision and a large brain, and is considered the most intelligent invertebrate. It even uses tools to build its den, which might feature a door that opens and closes!

HUMANS are large *vertebrates*.

Unlike fish, they must be taught to swim.

These large animals are not *indigenous* to the ocean.

They can't breathe underwater without special equipment.

Although some prey upon fish—which they capture to eat,

study, or keep in aquariums—if encountered in a reef,

most are harmless if they don't touch the coral

and other living ocean creatures.

1. SPOTTED CLEANER SHRIMP

2. ROCK BEAUTY

3. SPOTTED TRUNKFISH

4. BATWING CORAL CRAB

5. TRUMPETFISH

6. LONGSNOUT SEAHORSE

7. TWO-SPINED SEA STAR

8. SPOTTED MORAY EEL

9. RAINBOW PARROTFISH

10. FOUR-EYED BUTTERFLYFISH

11. FRENCH GRUNTS

12. QUEEN ANGELFISH

13. QUEEN TRIGGERFISH

14. REEF SHARK

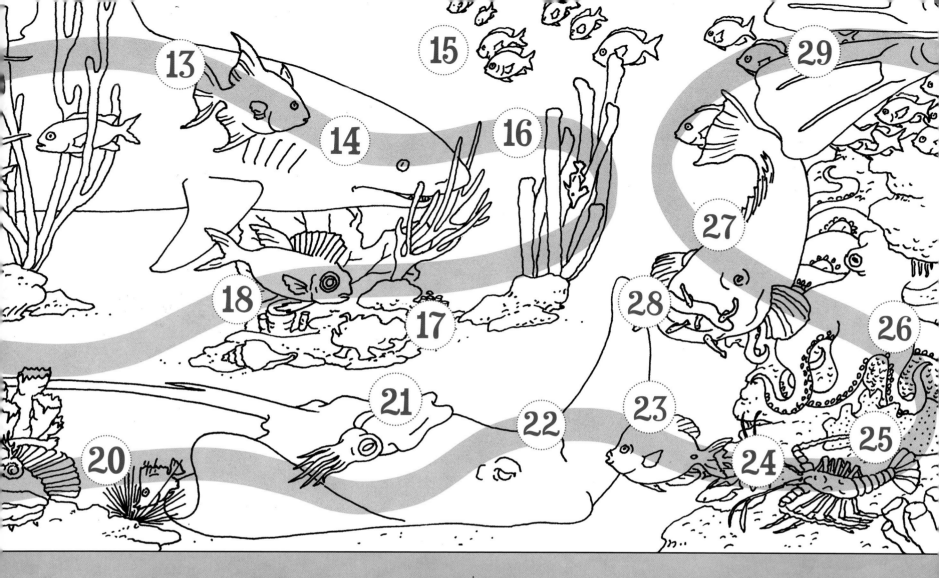

15. SERGEANT MAJORS

16. SLENDER FILEFISH

17. STRIATED FROGFISH

18. LONGSPINE SQUIRRELFISH

19. SPOTTED SCORPIONFISH

20. LONGSNOUT BUTTERFLYFISH

21. REEF SQUID

22. SOUTHERN STINGRAY

23. ATLANTIC BLUE TANG

24. FAIRY BASSLETS

25. SPINY LOBSTER

26. COMMON OCTOPUS

27. NASSAU GROUPER

28. YELLOW NOSE GOBIES

29. HUMAN

PROTECTING CORAL REEFS

Coral reefs are among the oldest and most fragile ecosystems on Earth. The water temperature in reefs usually stays constant throughout the year, but with climate change—caused in part by burning fossil fuels—that is changing. With even just a slight rise in temperature, the coral turns white—a process called bleaching—and dies. Greenhouse gases also cause water to become more acidic, which makes it harder for coral to grow. In addition, coral reefs are threatened by pollution, garbage and trash, oil spills, and pesticides, as well as by overfishing.

Because coral reefs are delicate and take so long to build, it is important that humans do everything we can to save them. Coral reefs are a source of nitrogen and other essential nutrients for marine food chains. Many of the fish we eat are either spawned or raised in coral reefs. They help protect shorelines from tropical storms. But most of all, we should care for coral reefs because they are irreplaceable living ecosystems that provide special homes for all sorts of unique creatures.

LEARN MORE ABOUT CORAL REEFS

Guides

Reef Fish Identification: Florida, Caribbean, Bahamas. Paul Humann and Ned DeLoach, New World Publications, Jacksonville, FL
Reef Coral Identification: Florida, Caribbean, Bahamas, including Marine Plants. Paul Humann and Ned DeLoach, New World Publications, Jacksonville, FL

Children's Books

Coral Reefs, Gail Gibbons, Holiday House, New York, NY
Coral Reefs, Seymour Simon, Harper, HarperCollins Publishers, New York, NY
Coral Reefs: A Journey Through an Aquatic World Full of Wonder, Jason Chin, Square Fish, A Neal Porter Book, Roaring Brook Press, New York, NY
Swim, Fish! Explore the Coral Reef, Susan B. Neuman, National Geographic Kids, Washington, DC
Coral Reefs, Kristin Baird Rattini, National Geographic Kids, Washington, DC
Coral Reefs: In Danger, by Samantha Brooke, illustrated by Peter Bull, Penguin Young Readers, New York, NY
Colorful Coral Reefs, Thea Feldman, Kingfisher Readers, New York, NY

Websites

University of Florida
    https://www.floridamuseum.ufl.edu/index.php/fish/home/
Sea and Sky
    http://www.seasky.org/coral-reef-life/coral-reef-fishes.html
Smithsonian (Ocean)
    https://ocean.si.edu/ecosystems/coral-reefs

Glossary

Camouflage: When an animal uses patterns, shapes, or colors to conceal itself by blending in with the background.

Cartilage: A tough, flexible tissue found in many animals that sometimes connects bones to muscles. Some animals, such as sharks, have skeletons made of cartilage instead of bones. Your nose and ears are made of cartilage.

Crustacean: An animal with a hard, external jointed skeleton, a pair of antennae, and appendages on each segment of its body. Most are marine animals. Crabs and lobsters are crustaceans.

Echinoderm: A creature with an internal skeleton. They have radial symmetry, tube feet, and often have five symmetrical "arms." Echinoderms include sea stars, sea urchins, and brittlestars.

Indigenous: Living or occurring naturally in a particular place or location; native or original to an area.

Invertebrate: Any of the large number of animals without backbones. Some have soft bodies, like a worm, or a hard, exterior shell, like a lobster.

Mollusk: An invertebrate with a soft body. Usually mollusks are found in water or wet environments. Some have hard exterior shells. Snails, oysters, and clams are mollusks, and so are octopi and squid.

Monogamous: An animal who has only one mate at a time is called "monogamous."

Parasite: A creature that lives in, with, or on another creature for nourishment or protection, but doesn't necessarily help the other, and may even harm it.

Predator: An animal that hunts, catches, and eats other animals.

Territorial: When a creature prefers and defends a particular area from others. It could be on land, in water, or even an area of the sky.

Venomous: Able to inflict a sting or bite to deliver chemicals, like poison, that can kill or paralyze other animals.

Vertebrate: An animal with a spinal column, or backbone, and a brain enclosed in a skull. Fish, amphibians, reptiles, birds, and mammals are all vertebrates.

Index

Page numbers in italic type refer to illustrations.

anemones 4, 6
angelfish
    dwarf, 6
    queen, 16, *16–17*, 34
    rock beauty, 6, *6–7*

basslets
    fairy, 28, *28–29*, 35
butterflyfish, 6
    four–eyed, 14, *14*, 34
    longsnout, 25, *25*, 35

camouflage, 8, 21, 22, 25, 26, 36
cartilage, 19, 27, 36
clams, 27, 30
coral bleaching, 36
crabs 19, 34, 36
    batwing, 8, *8–9*, 34
crustaceans, 6, *6*, 8, *8–9*, 25, 36

echinoderms, 11, 36

filefish
    fringed, 21
    orange–spotted, 21
    pygmy, 21
    scrawled, 21
    slender, 21, *21*, 35
    unicorn, 21
frogfish
    striated, 22, *23*, 25, 35

groupers
    goliath, 30, *30*
    Nassau, 30, *30–33*, 35
gobies
    yellow nose, 30, *30*, 35
grunts
    French, *2–5*, 14, *14–19*, 34

indigenous, 32, 36
invertebrates, 25, 36

lobsters, 8, 36
    spiny, 28, *29*, 35

mollusks, 27, 30, 36
monogamous, 6, 36
moray eels, 11, 22
    goldentail, 11
    green, 11
    honeycomb, 11
    purple mouth, 11
    spotted, *10–11*, 11, 34
    stout, 11
    viper, 11

octopi, 4, 6
    common, *28–30*, 30, 35

parasites, 6, 16–17, 30
parrotfish
    rainbow, 12, *12–13*, 34
polyps, 4
predators, 8, 14, 16, 19, 22, 25, 27, 28
prey, 8, 16, 19, 26, 30

rock beauties, 6, *6–7*, 34

scorpion fish
    spotted, *24*, 25, 35
seahorses, 11
    longsnout, *10*, 11, 34
sea stars (also called starfish), 4, 11, 36
    two–spined, *10*, 11, 34
sea urchins, 4, 25, 38
sergeant majors, 20, *20–21*, *32–33*, 35
sharks, 8, 27
    great hammerhead, 19
    nurse, 19
    reef, *15–20*, 19, 34
    sand tiger, 19
    whale, 19
shrimp, 8
    spotted cleaner shrimp, 6, *6*, 34

sponges, 4, 8, *8–9*
    pipe sponge, 8, *8–9*
squids, 30, 36
    reef, 26, *26–27*, 35
squirrelfish,
    longspine, 22, *22–23*, 35
stingrays
    southern, *26–27*, 27, 35

tangs
    Atlantic blue, 28, *28*, 35
territorial, 6, 36
triggerfish
    queen, 19, *19–20*, 34
trumpetfish, *4*, *7*, 8, *9*, 34
trunkfish
    spotted, 8, *8–9*, 34
tube worms, 4, 25

venomous, 27, 36
vertebrates 32, 36